HEINEMANN FIRST ATLAS

Daniel Block and Marta Segal Block

Heinemann LIBRARY

www.heinemann.co.uk/library
Visit our website to find out more information about Heinemann Library books.

To order:
 Phone 44 (0) 1865 888066
 Send a fax to 44 (0) 1865 314091
💻 Visit the Heinemann Bookshop at www.heinemann.co.uk/library to browse our catalogue and order online.

First published in Great Britain by Heinemann, Halley Court, Jordan Hill, Oxford, OX2 8EJ, part of Harcourt Education.
Raintree is a registered trademark of Harcourt Education Ltd.

Editorial: Andrew Farrow, Vicki Yates, and Diyan Leake
Design: Richard Parker and Manhattan Design
Picture Research: Hannah Taylor
Production: Duncan Gilbert

Originated by Chroma Graphics (Overseas) Pte. Ltd
Printed and bound in China by WKT Co. Ltd

10 digit ISBN 0 431 90659 9 (hardback)
13 digit ISBN 978 0431 90659 1
11 10 09 08 07
10 9 8 7 6 5 4 3 2 1

10 digit ISBN 0 431 90660 2 (paperback)
13 digit ISBN 978 0431 90660 7
11 10 09 08 07
10 9 8 7 6 5 4 3 2 1

British Library Cataloguing in Publication Data
Block, Daniel
Heinemann First Atlas
912
A full catalogue record for this book is available from the British Library.

Acknowledgements
The publishers would like to thank the following for permission to reproduce photographs: Alamy Images/John Henshall: p. **5** bottom; istockphoto: p. **4** bottom left; Lonely Planet Images/Richard I'Anson: p. **5** top; Science Photo Library/NASA/Goddard Space Flight Centre: p. **4** top right; Woodfall Wild Images/David Woodfall: p. **5** middle.

Cover photograph of the Earth from space reproduced with permission of Science Photo Library/NASA/Goddard Space Flight Centre.

Map illustrations created by International Mapping Associates.

Every effort has been made to contact copyright holders of any material reproduced in this book. Any omissions will be rectified in subsequent printings if notice is given to the publishers.

Contents

What is a globe?

A globe is a ball-shaped map.
It is a model of the Earth.

What is a map?

A map is a flat drawing of a part of the Earth. Maps have pictures on them called symbols.

City

River

Mountain

Key

The key on a map explains what the different symbols mean.

Scale

The scale tells you how far apart things on the map are in real life.

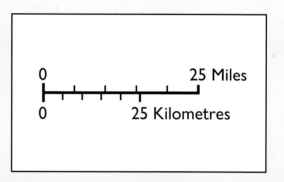

Compass rose

The compass rose shows the directions on a map.

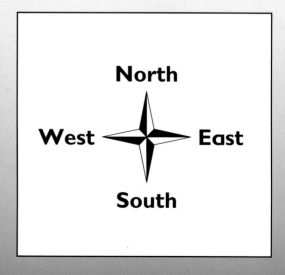

What are maps for?

Maps can help you find places.
They can help you find a fire station or a school.

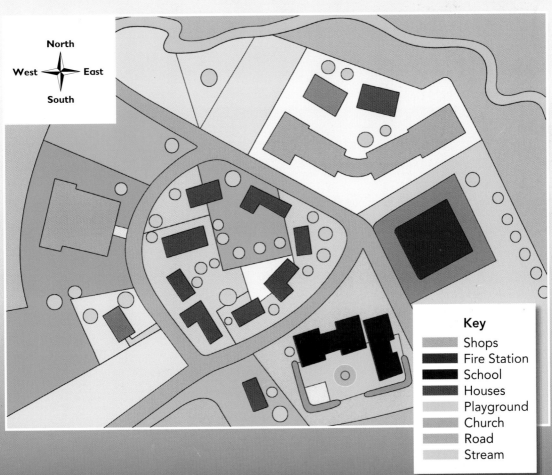

North

West ✦ East

South

Key	
	Shops
	Fire Station
	School
	Houses
	Playground
	Church
	Road
	Stream

The world

This map shows the whole world.
It shows where the seven continents are.

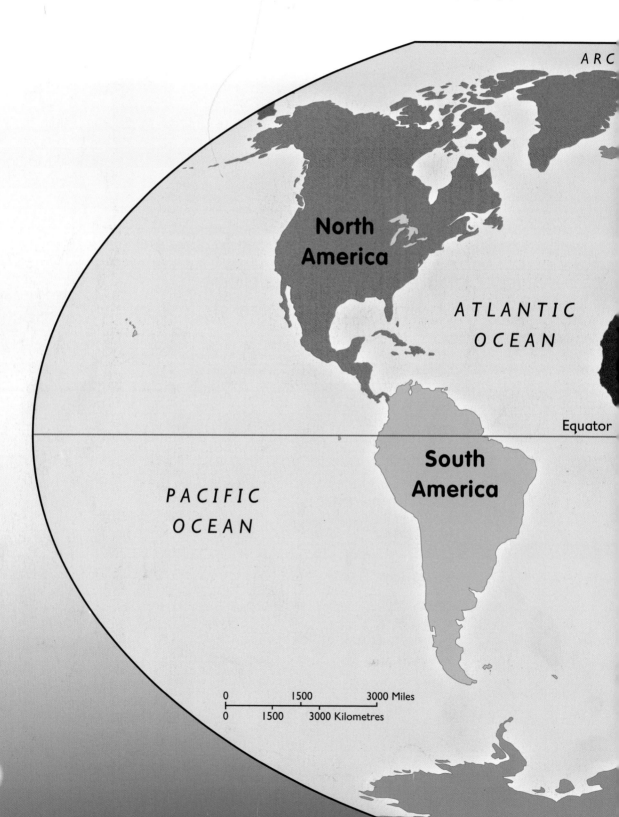

It also shows the oceans.

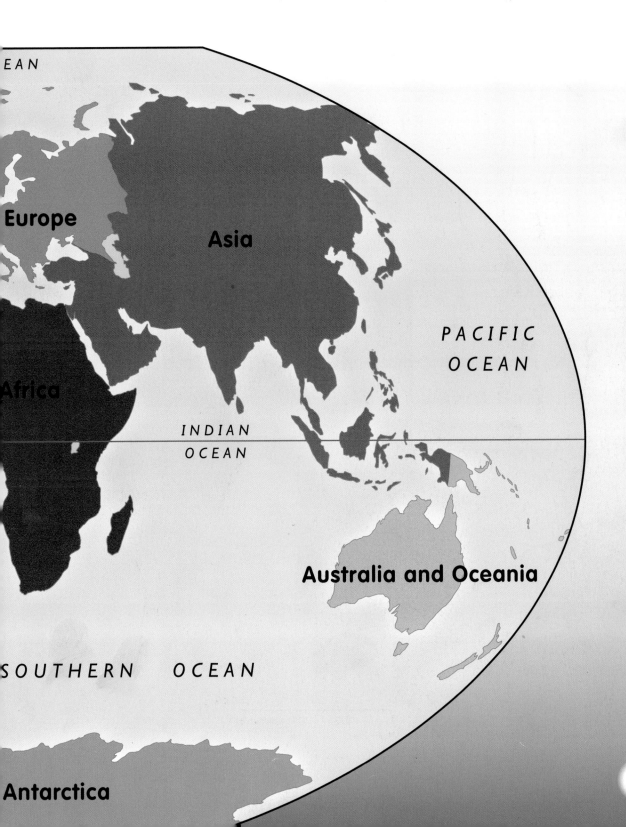

Land and water

Maps can show where mountains and deserts are.

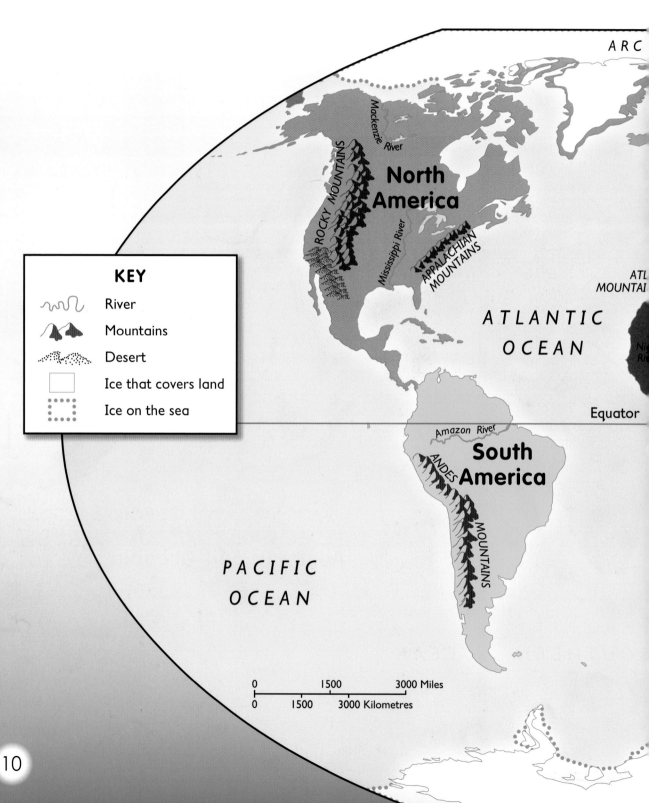

KEY

~~~ River

🌋 Mountains

⛰ Desert

☐ Ice that covers land

⬚ Ice on the sea

ARC

Mackenzie River

North America

ROCKY MOUNTAINS

Mississippi River

APPALACHIAN MOUNTAINS

ATL MOUNTAI

ATLANTIC OCEAN

Ni Ri

Equator

Amazon River

South America

ANDES

MOUNTAINS

PACIFIC OCEAN

| 0 | 1500 | 3000 Miles |
| 0 | 1500 | 3000 Kilometres |

They can show rivers and lakes.

Climate

Climate is the usual pattern of weather that there is in a place.

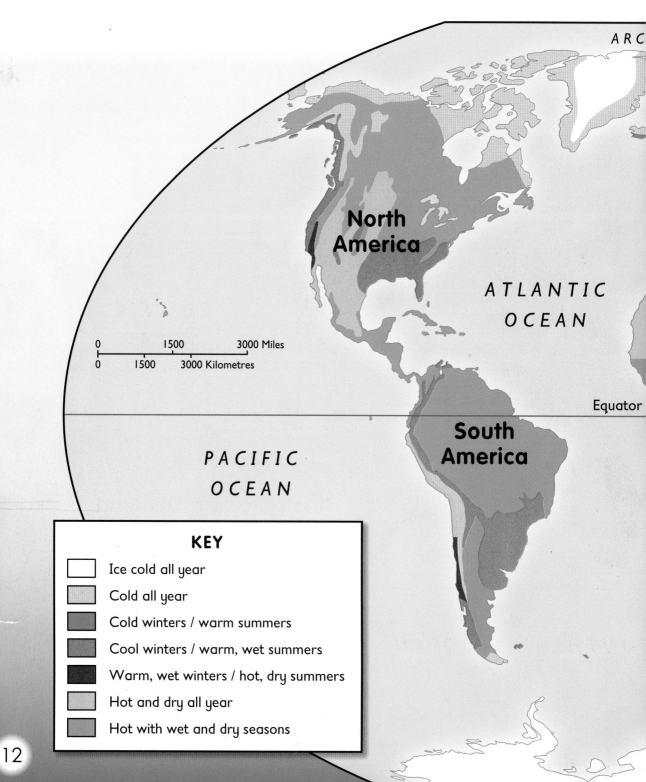

ARC

North
America

ATLANTIC
OCEAN

0   1500   3000 Miles
0   1500   3000 Kilometres

Equator

South
America

PACIFIC
OCEAN

KEY

- Ice cold all year
- Cold all year
- Cold winters / warm summers
- Cool winters / warm, wet summers
- Warm, wet winters / hot, dry summers
- Hot and dry all year
- Hot with wet and dry seasons

Maps can show what the climate
is like in different parts of the world.

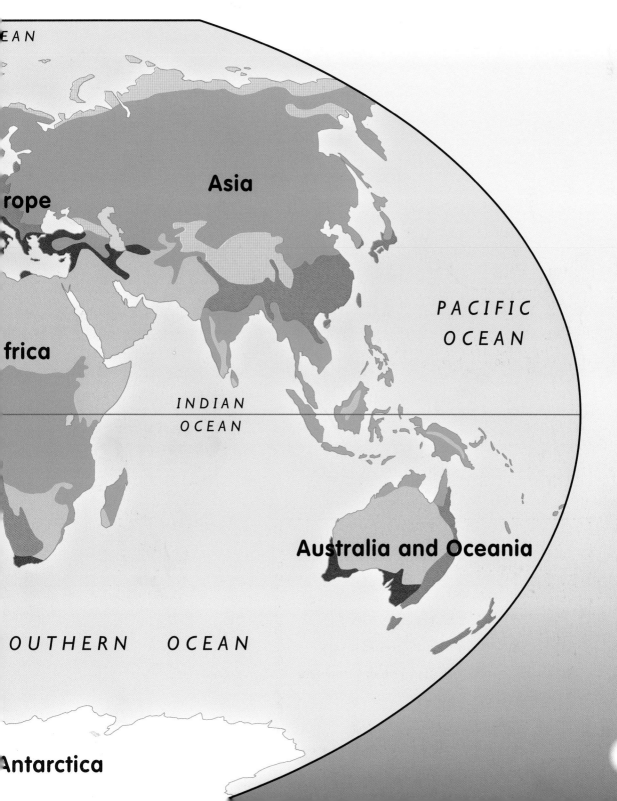

Countries of the world

This map shows some of the countries of the world.

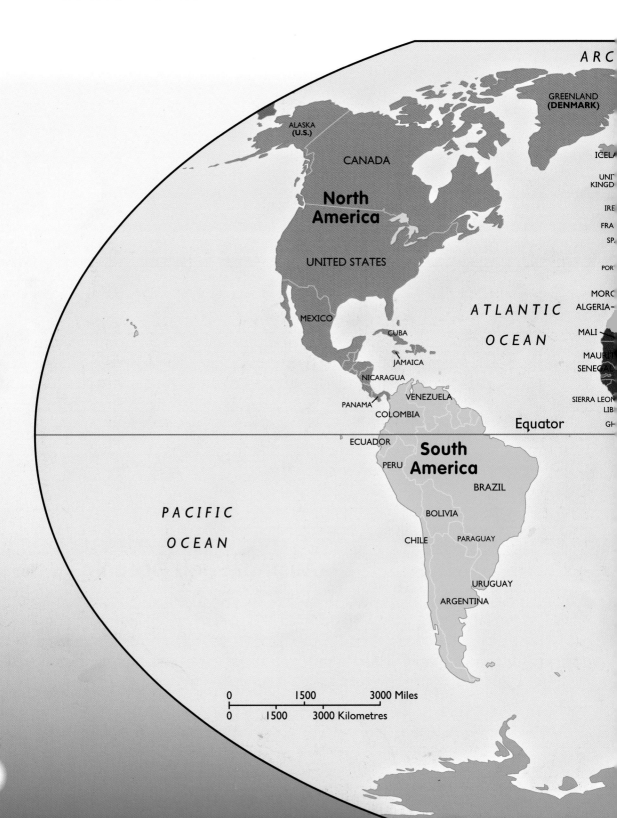

ARC

GREENLAND
(DENMARK)

ICELA

UNIT
KINGD

IRE

FRA

SP

POR

MORC

ALGERIA

MALI

MAURIT

SENEGAL

SIERRA LEON

LIB

GH

ALASKA
(U.S.)

CANADA

North America

UNITED STATES

MEXICO

CUBA

JAMAICA

NICARAGUA

PANAMA

COLOMBIA

VENEZUELA

ATLANTIC

OCEAN

Equator

ECUADOR

PERU

South America

BRAZIL

BOLIVIA

CHILE

PARAGUAY

URUGUAY

ARGENTINA

PACIFIC

OCEAN

0	1500	3000 Miles
0	1500	3000 Kilometres

Which continents have lots of countries?

The British Isles

This map shows the different parts of the United Kingdom.

Shetland Islands

Orkney Islands

Outer Hebrides

NORTH SEA

ATLANTIC OCEAN

Scotland

UNITED KINGDOM

Northern Ireland

Isle of Man

REPUBLIC OF IRELAND

IRISH SEA

England

Wales

CELTIC SEA

Isle of Wight

English Channel

Channel Islands

FRANCE

0   100   200 Miles
0   100   200 Kilometres

This map shows some of the cities and towns in the British Isles.

KEY

⊕ Capital

★ Main city

● Large city

• City or town

ATLANTIC OCEAN

NORTH SEA

Scotland

• Aberdeen

Glasgow • ★ Edinburgh

Northern Ireland

★ Belfast

Newcastle upon Tyne

Sunderland

England

IRISH SEA

Leeds • York

Bradford

Preston

Dublin ⊕

Liverpool • Manchester

REPUBLIC OF IRELAND

Kingston upon Hull

Sheffield

Stoke-on-Trent

Nottingham

Derby

Wolverhampton

Leicester

Norwich

Birmingham

Coventry

Cork •

Wales

Milton Keynes • Luton

Swansea •

Reading •

London ⊕

CELTIC SEA

★ Cardiff • Bristol

Dover •

Southampton

Plymouth •

English Channel

0   100   200 Miles
0   100   200 Kilometres

FRANCE

Europe

There are many countries in Europe.

Some countries are big and some
are small.

KEY

✪	Capital
●	City
〰	River
⛰	Mountains

RUSSIA

URAL MOUNTAINS

★ Moscow

Ural River

Asia

KAZAKHSTAN

RUS

iev

RAINE

OVA

CAUCASUS MOUNTAINS

Caspian Sea

Black Sea

GEORGIA

AZERBAIJAN

RIA

anbul

RKEY

0	200	400 Miles
0	200	400 Kilometres

Rivers and mountains

This map shows some of the rivers and mountains in Europe.

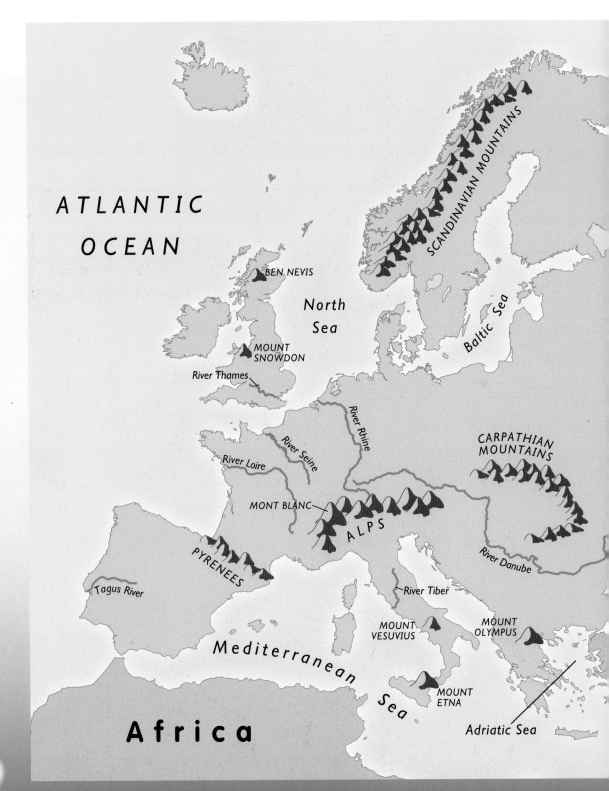

ATLANTIC OCEAN

BEN NEVIS

North Sea

SCANDINAVIAN MOUNTAINS

Baltic Sea

MOUNT SNOWDON

River Thames

River Rhine

River Seine

River Loire

CARPATHIAN MOUNTAINS

MONT BLANC

ALPS

River Danube

PYRENEES

Tagus River

River Tiber

MOUNT VESUVIUS

MOUNT OLYMPUS

Mediterranean Sea

MOUNT ETNA

Adriatic Sea

Africa

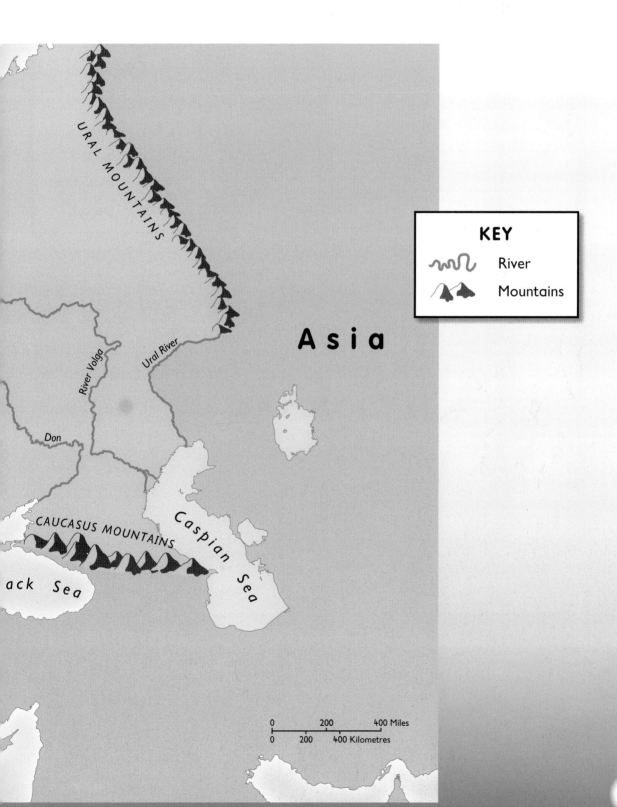

URAL MOUNTAINS

River Volga

Ural River

Don

Asia

KEY

River

Mountains

CAUCASUS MOUNTAINS

Caspian Sea

ack Sea

| 0 | 200 | 400 Miles |
| 0 | 200 | 400 Kilometres |

North America

North America has some very big countries.
There are also some smaller countries.

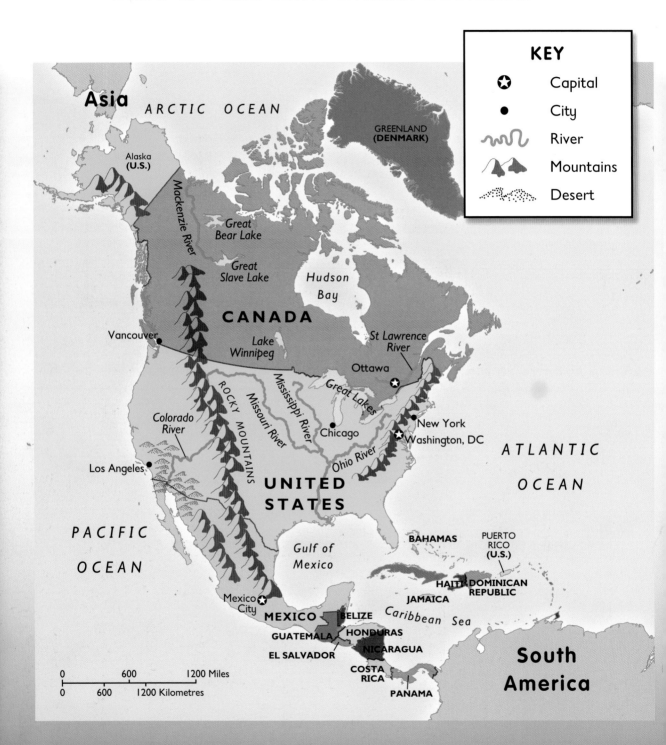

KEY

⭐ Capital
● City
〰️ River
⛰️ Mountains
Desert

South America

The wet Amazon rainforest is in South America.
So is the dry Atacama Desert.

North America

Caribbean Sea

Caracas

VENEZUELA

Georgetown

Paramaribo

FRENCH GUIANA (FRANCE)

Orinoco River

COLOMBIA

GUYANA

SURINAME

Bogotá

Quito

Equator

ECUADOR

Amazon River

Galápagos Islands (ECUADOR)

PERU

BRAZIL

Lima

PACIFIC OCEAN

La Paz

Brasília

BOLIVIA

Sucre

Paraná River

Lake Titicaca

PARAGUAY

Rio de Janeiro

São Paulo

Asunción

Atacama Desert

ANDES MOUNTAINS

0   400   800 Miles
0   400   800 Kilometres

CHILE

URUGUAY

Santiago

Buenos Aires

Montevideo

ARGENTINA

ATLANTIC OCEAN

Falkland Islands (UNITED KINGDOM)

KEY

✪ Capital

● City

〜 River

⛰ Mountains

⋯ Desert

🌳 Rainforest

Africa

Africa is a large continent with many countries. The huge Sahara Desert is in Africa.

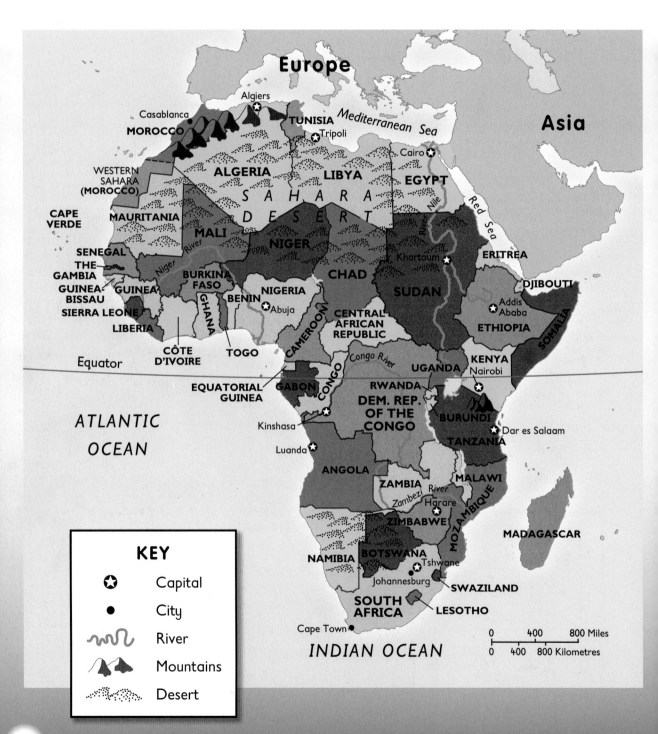

KEY

✪	Capital
•	City
〜	River
⛰	Mountains
⋰⋱	Desert

Australia and Oceania

Australia is both a continent and a country. Oceania is the area that includes Australia and the islands close to it.

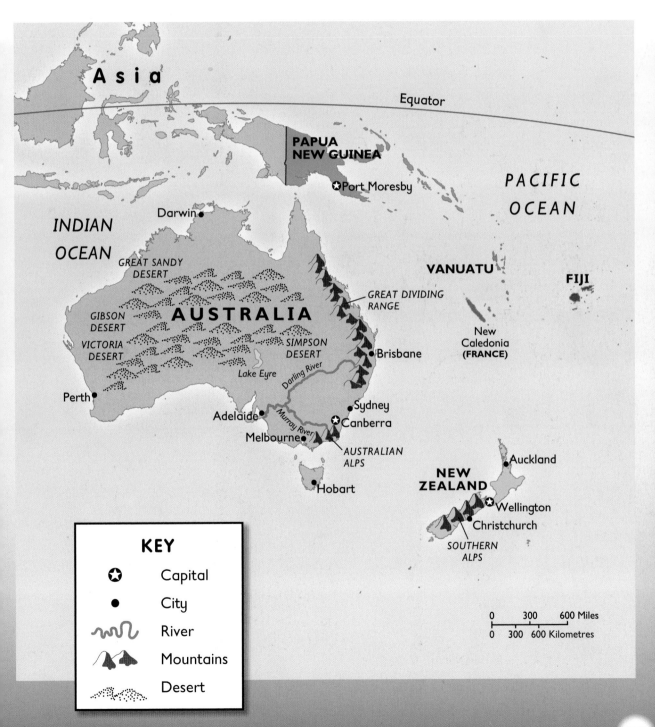

Asia

Equator

PAPUA
NEW GUINEA

★ Port Moresby

PACIFIC
OCEAN

Darwin •

INDIAN
OCEAN

GREAT SANDY
DESERT

VANUATU

FIJI

GIBSON
DESERT

AUSTRALIA

GREAT DIVIDING
RANGE

New
Caledonia
(FRANCE)

VICTORIA
DESERT

SIMPSON
DESERT

• Brisbane

Lake Eyre

Darling River

Perth •

Sydney
Adelaide •
Murray River
★ Canberra

Melbourne •

Auckland •

AUSTRALIAN
ALPS

NEW
ZEALAND

Hobart •

★ Wellington
• Christchurch

SOUTHERN
ALPS

KEY

★	Capital
•	City
∿	River
⛰	Mountains
⠿	Desert

0   300   600 Miles

0   300   600 Kilometres

Asia

Asia is the largest continent.

ARCTIC OCEAN

Europe

R U S S I A

Ob River

Mediterranean Sea

Black Sea

Ankara

TURKEY   GEORGIA

CYPRUS   ARMENIA

LEBANON

Jerusalem

SYRIA

PALESTINE

IRAQ

Baku

AZERBAIJAN

ISRAEL

JORDAN

Baghdad

Tehran

Caspian Sea

Ural River

K A Z A K H S T A N

Aral Sea

UZBEKISTAN

TURKMENISTAN

KYRGYZSTAN

TAJIKISTAN

BHUT

NEPAL

IRAN

SAUDI
ARABIA

KUWAIT

Persian Gulf

Mecca   Riyadh

QATAR

AFGHANISTAN

Kabul

Islamabad

Indus R.

Lahore

PAKISTAN

New
Delhi

Karachi

River Ganges

Africa

Red Sea

UNITED ARAB
EMIRATES   Muscat

OMAN

Sanaa

YEMEN

Mumbai

INDIA

Dha

BANGLADES

Bay o
Benga

SRI LANKA

Colombo

INDIAN OCEAN

0   500   1000 Miles

0   500   1000 Kilometres

More people live in Asia than
on any other continent.

KEY

★	Capital
●	City
〰	River
⛰	Mountains
⠒	Desert

Lena River

Lake Baikal

MONGOLIA

Ulaanbaatar

NORTH KOREA

Pyongyang

Seoul

SOUTH KOREA

Tokyo

JAPAN

Huang He

Beijing

CHINA

Shanghai

Chang Jiang

TAIWAN

Hong Kong

Mekong River

PACIFIC

OCEAN

MYANMAR / BURMA

Hanoi

South China Sea

Manila

PHILIPPINES

Yangon

LAOS

VIETNAM

THAILAND

Bangkok

CAMBODIA

Phnom Penh

MALAYSIA

Kuala Lumpur

SINGAPORE

I N D O N E S I A

Jakarta

The Arctic

The North Pole is covered in ice.
There is no land at the North Pole.

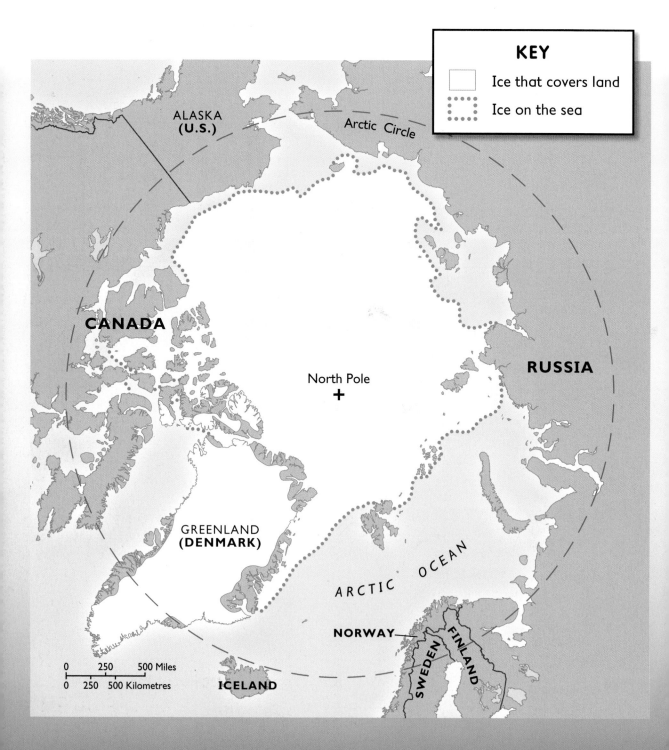

KEY
- Ice that covers land
- Ice on the sea

ALASKA (U.S.)

Arctic Circle

CANADA

RUSSIA

North Pole
+

GREENLAND (DENMARK)

ARCTIC OCEAN

NORWAY

0   250   500 Miles
0   250   500 Kilometres

ICELAND

SWEDEN

FINLAND

Antarctica

Antarctica is the coldest continent.
All the land is covered in very thick ice.

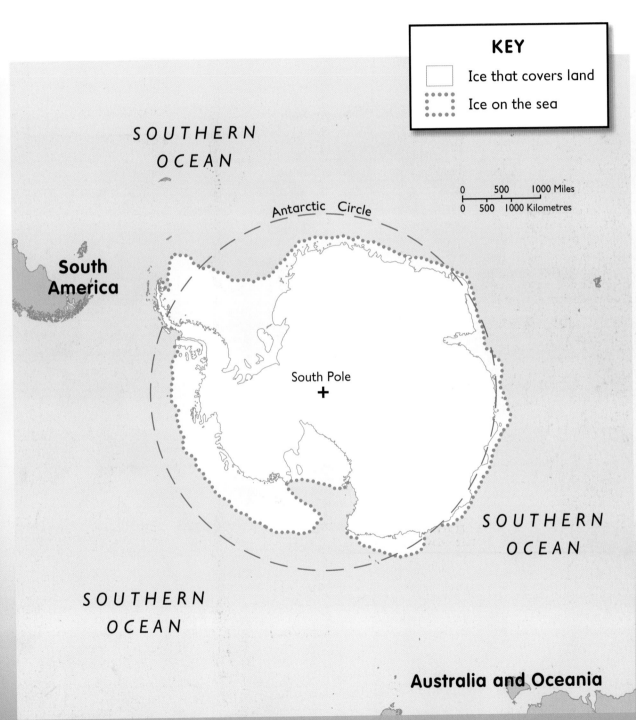

KEY

☐ Ice that covers land

⋯ Ice on the sea

SOUTHERN OCEAN

0   500   1000 Miles
0   500   1000 Kilometres

Antarctic Circle

South America

South Pole
+

SOUTHERN OCEAN

SOUTHERN OCEAN

Australia and Oceania

Lines around the world

Maps have lines that help to show where places are.
The Equator is halfway between the North Pole and the South Pole.

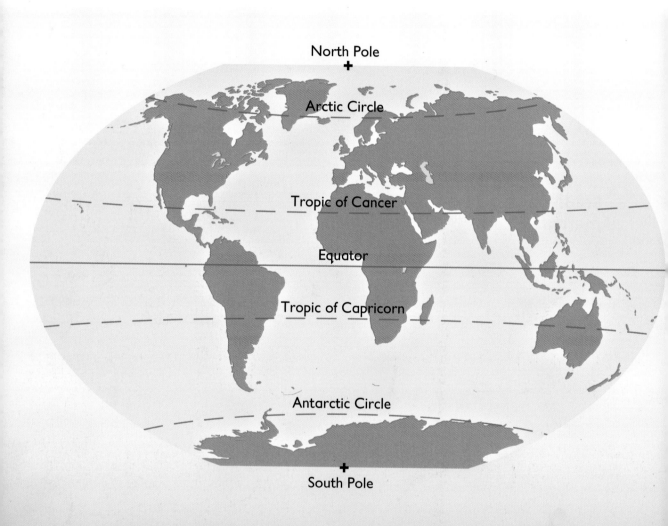

Glossary

capital

most important city in a country

continent

one of the very large areas of land on the Earth

desert

area of land where it hardly ever rains

North Pole

the point on the Earth that is as far north as you can go

rainforest

thick forest that grows in hot, wet places

South Pole

the point on the Earth that is as far south as you can go

Index

This is a list of some of the places in this atlas.